Apr. 2013

WITHDRAWN

NEW MEXICO

Julie Murray

EXPLORE THE UNITED STATES ★ EXPLORE THE UNITED STATES ★ EXPLORE THE UNITED STATES ★ EXPLORE THE UNITED STATES

Big Buddy BOOKS

Explore the United States

VISIT US AT
www.abdopublishing.com

Published by ABDO Publishing Company, PO Box 398166, Minneapolis, MN 55439.

Copyright © 2013 by Abdo Consulting Group, Inc. International copyrights reserved in all countries. No part of this book may be reproduced in any form without written permission from the publisher. Big Buddy Books™ is a trademark and logo of ABDO Publishing Company.

Printed in the United States of America, North Mankato, Minnesota.
042012
092012

♻ PRINTED ON RECYCLED PAPER

Coordinating Series Editor: Rochelle Baltzer
Editor: Sarah Tieck
Contributing Editors: Megan M. Gunderson, BreAnn Rumsch, Marcia Zappa
Graphic Design: Adam Craven
Cover Photograph: *Shutterstock*: Michelle Dulieu.
Interior Photographs/Illustrations: *AP Photo*: North Wind Picture Archives via AP Images (pp. 13, 27), Phillips Collection (p. 23), Roswell Daily Record Mark Wilson (p. 27), Jake Schoellkopf (p. 27), Ted S. Warren (p. 25); *Getty Images*: Michael Nichols/National Geographic (p. 21); *Glow Images*: Imagebroker RM (p. 19); *iStockphoto*: ©iStockphoto.com/PhilAugustavo (p. 19), ©iStockphoto.com/itakefotos4u (p. 30), ©iStockphoto.com/jzabloski (p. 30), ©iStockphoto.com/tmarvin (p. 30); *Shutterstock*: Rusty Dodson (p. 29), Dr_Flash (p. 26), Jeffrey M. Frank (p. 11), David James (p. 9), Philip Lange (p. 30), a. v. ley (p. 5), Caitlin Mirra (p. 9), Ken Schulze (p. 17), Harris Shiffman (p. 26).

All population figures taken from the 2010 US census.

Library of Congress Cataloging-in-Publication Data

Murray, Julie, 1969-
 New Mexico / Julie Murray.
   p. cm. -- (Explore the United States)
 ISBN 978-1-61783-369-4
 1. New Mexico--Juvenile literature. I. Title.
 F796.3.M87 2013
 978.9--dc23
                            2012010555

Contents

One Nation

The United States is a **diverse** country. It has farmland, cities, coasts, and mountains. Its people come from many different backgrounds. And, its history covers more than 200 years.

Today the country includes 50 states. New Mexico is one of these states. Let's learn more about New Mexico and its story!

Did You Know?

New Mexico became a state on January 6, 1912. It was the forty-seventh state to join the nation.

New Mexico is known for its colorful, rocky landscape.

5

NEW MEXICO UP CLOSE

The United States has four main **regions**. New Mexico is in the West.

New Mexico has four states on its borders. Arizona is west. Colorado is north. Oklahoma is east. Texas is east and south. The country of Mexico is south.

New Mexico is the fifth-largest state. Its total area is 121,590 square miles (314,917 sq km). About 2 million people live there.

REGIONS OF THE UNITED STATES

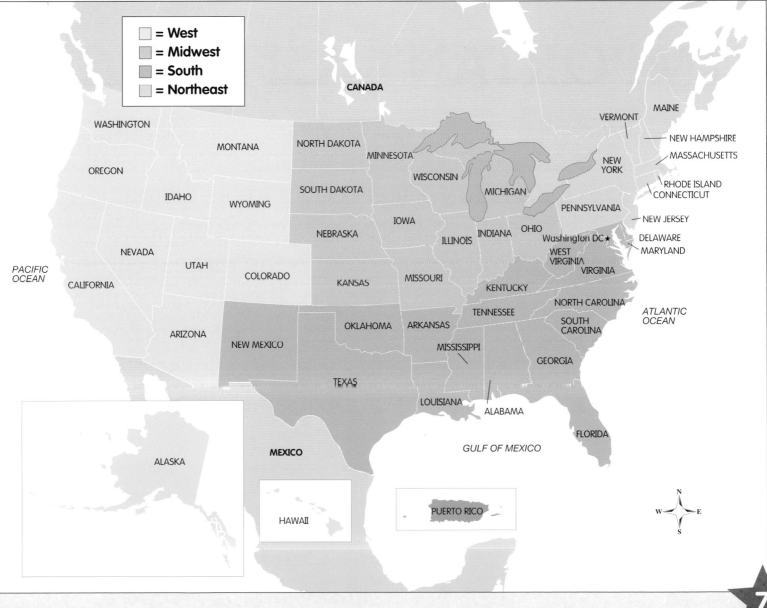

Legend:
- ☐ = West
- ☐ = Midwest
- ☐ = South
- ☐ = Northeast

CANADA

WASHINGTON

MONTANA

NORTH DAKOTA

MINNESOTA

VERMONT

MAINE

NEW HAMPSHIRE

MASSACHUSETTS

OREGON

IDAHO

WYOMING

SOUTH DAKOTA

WISCONSIN

MICHIGAN

NEW YORK

RHODE ISLAND

CONNECTICUT

PENNSYLVANIA

IOWA

NEVADA

UTAH

NEBRASKA

ILLINOIS

INDIANA

OHIO

Washington DC ★

NEW JERSEY

DELAWARE

MARYLAND

WEST VIRGINIA

VIRGINIA

PACIFIC OCEAN

CALIFORNIA

COLORADO

KANSAS

MISSOURI

KENTUCKY

NORTH CAROLINA

ATLANTIC OCEAN

ARIZONA

NEW MEXICO

OKLAHOMA

ARKANSAS

TENNESSEE

SOUTH CAROLINA

MISSISSIPPI

GEORGIA

TEXAS

LOUISIANA

ALABAMA

FLORIDA

GULF OF MEXICO

ALASKA

MEXICO

HAWAII

PUERTO RICO

N W E S

7

IMPORTANT CITIES

Santa Fe is New Mexico's **capital**. It is one of the oldest cities in the United States. It is known for its historic buildings. Also, Santa Fe is home to many artists.

Albuquerque (AL-buh-kuhr-kee) is the largest city in the state. It is home to 545,852 people. The city is located along a river called the Rio Grande. Its history dates to the 1700s. Today, it is home to many businesses. It also hosts events, such as a hot air balloon festival.

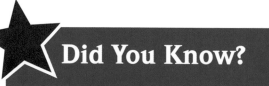

Did You Know?

The Palace of the Governors is one of the nation's oldest government buildings. It was built in the 1600s as a home to the Spanish government. Today, it is a museum in Santa Fe.

The New Mexico Capitol is called "the Roundhouse." It is the country's only round capitol building!

New Mexico

★ Santa Fe
Rio Rancho ● ●Albuquerque

●Las Cruces

The Albuquerque International Balloon Fiesta takes place every October. It is one of the world's largest hot air balloon festivals!

Las Cruces (lahs-KROO-says) is New Mexico's second-largest city. It is home to 97,618 people. It is located near the Organ Mountains. It is also near a rocket-testing center.

Rio Rancho is the third-largest city in the state. It has 87,521 people. The city is home to many businesses. Intel computers are one important product made there.

The US government tests rockets at the White Sands Missile Range near Las Cruces.

New Mexico in History

New Mexico's history includes Native Americans and settlers. The Mogollon and Ancestral Pueblo peoples were two main tribes in the area. They lived off New Mexico's land for thousands of years.

Around 1530, the Spanish were the first Europeans to explore the area. The population grew as more and more settlers arrived. New Mexico became a state in 1912.

Some Ancestral Pueblos carved their homes out of cliffs. These cliff dwellings kept them safe from attacks by other tribes.

Timeline

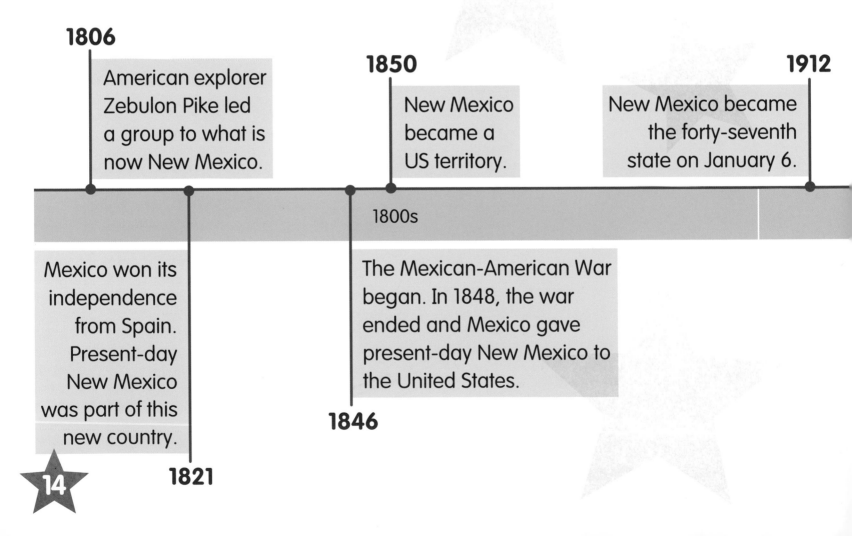

1806

American explorer Zebulon Pike led a group to what is now New Mexico.

1850

New Mexico became a US territory.

1912

New Mexico became the forty-seventh state on January 6.

1800s

Mexico won its independence from Spain. Present-day New Mexico was part of this new country.

The Mexican-American War began. In 1848, the war ended and Mexico gave present-day New Mexico to the United States.

1846

1821

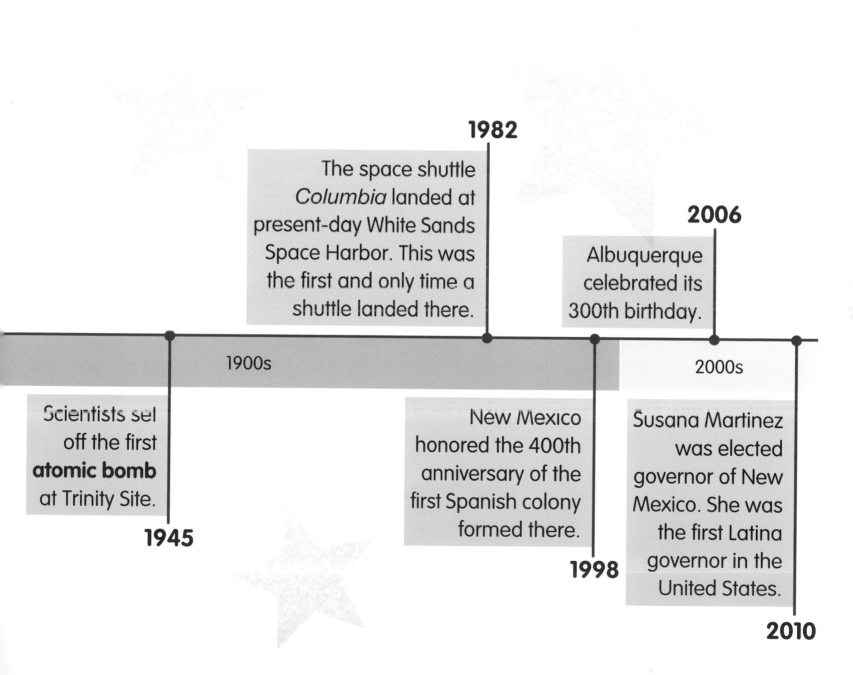

1982

The space shuttle *Columbia* landed at present-day White Sands Space Harbor. This was the first and only time a shuttle landed there.

2006

Albuquerque celebrated its 300th birthday.

1900s

2000s

Scientists set off the first **atomic bomb** at Trinity Site.

New Mexico honored the 400th anniversary of the first Spanish colony formed there.

Susana Martinez was elected governor of New Mexico. She was the first Latina governor in the United States.

1945

1998

2010

ACROSS THE LAND

New Mexico has deserts, mountains, forests, valleys, caves, and grassy areas. It has five major rivers, including the Rio Grande. The Rocky Mountains are in northern New Mexico.

Many types of animals make their homes in New Mexico. These include black bears, roadrunners, coyotes, rattlesnakes, and mountain lions.

Did You Know?

In July, the average temperature in New Mexico is 74°F (23°C). In January, it is 34°F (1°C).

The Rio Grande flows down the middle of New Mexico.

Earning a Living

Many government workers live in New Mexico. Some are scientists, and others work for the military.

The weather, natural beauty, art, and history of New Mexico make it a popular vacation spot. So, some people have jobs helping visitors.

New Mexico has many natural **resources**. **Minerals** from the state are used to provide power. New Mexico has limited water and poor soil, so few crops are grown there. But, livestock is raised on the land. This includes beef cattle.

★★★★★★★★★★★★★★★★★★★★★★★★

Wells in New Mexico collect oil from deep under the ground.

★★★★★★★★★★★★★★★★★★★★★★★★

Cattle graze on the state's wide-open stretches of land.

19

Natural Wonder

Carlsbad Caverns National Park is in southeastern New Mexico. It has more than 80 caves! They formed over millions of years and continue to change today.

Below ground, there are more than 100 miles (160 km) of cave passages! People can tour some of them. Above ground, people can see native plants and animals.

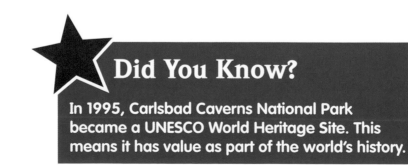

Did You Know?

In 1995, Carlsbad Caverns National Park became a UNESCO World Heritage Site. This means it has value as part of the world's history.

Lechuguilla Cave is part of Carlsbad Caverns National Park. It is one of the world's longest known caves!

HOMETOWN HEROES

Many famous people have lived in New Mexico. Painter Georgia O'Keeffe was born in Wisconsin in 1887. But, she spent many years in New Mexico. She began regularly visiting the state in 1929 and moved there in 1949.

O'Keeffe is one of the best-known American artists. She often found ideas for her paintings from studying New Mexico's land.

Did You Know?

The Georgia O'Keeffe Museum is in Santa Fe.

O'Keeffe painted in New Mexico almost every year from 1929 until her death in 1986.

Jeff Bezos was born in Albuquerque in 1964. He is the founder and **chief executive officer** of Amazon.com. This famous online store sells books, DVDs, CDs, and many other products.

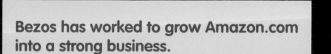

Bezos has worked to grow Amazon.com into a strong business.

25

Tour Book

Do you want to go to New Mexico? If you visit the state, here are some places to go and things to do!

★ Splash

Go white-water rafting on the Rio Grande! This is a popular adventure for visitors.

★ Taste

Try spicy red or green chiles grown in New Mexico. Native American fry bread and Mexican tamales are also popular foods in the state.

★ Remember

Visit Ancestral Pueblo dwellings. Some are thousands of years old!

★ Cheer

See a University of New Mexico basketball game. These are held at the popular University Arena, known as "the Pit."

★ Discover

Visit the International UFO Museum in Roswell. Some people believe aliens in a UFO crashed near Roswell in 1947.

A GREAT STATE

The story of New Mexico is important to the United States. The people and places that make up this state offer something special to the country. Together with all the states, New Mexico helps make the United States great.

White Sands National Monument has sandy land shaped by wind.

Fast Facts

Date of Statehood:
January 6, 1912

Population (rank):
2,059,179
(36th most-populated state)

Total Area (rank):
121,590 square miles
(5th largest state)

Motto:
"Crescit Eundo"
(It Grows As It Goes)

Nickname:
Land of Enchantment

State Capital:
Santa Fe

Flag:

Flower: Yucca Flower

Postal Abbreviation:
NM

Tree: Piñon Pine

Bird: Roadrunner

Important Words

atomic bomb a bomb that uses the energy of atoms. Atoms are tiny particles that make up matter.

capital a city where government leaders meet.

chief executive officer the leader of a company.

diverse made up of things that are different from each other.

mineral a natural substance. Minerals make up rocks and other parts of nature.

region a large part of a country that is different from other parts.

resource a supply of something useful or valued.

Web Sites

To learn more about New Mexico, visit ABDO Publishing Company online. Web sites about New Mexico are featured on our Book Links page. These links are routinely monitored and updated to provide the most current information available.

www.abdopublishing.com

Index